SCHOLASTIC

READ & RESP

C000215532

Bringing the best books to life in the classroom

Activities based on **Goodnight Mister Tom**

By Michelle Magorian

Terms and conditions

IMPORTANT – PERMITTED USE AND WARNINGS – READ CAREFULLY BEFORE USING

Copyright in the software contained in this CD-ROM and in its accompanying material belongs to Scholastic Limited. All rights reserved. © 2016 Scholastic Ltd.

Save for these purposes, or as expressly authorised in the accompanying materials, the software may not be copied, reproduced, used, sold, licensed, transferred, exchanged, hired, or exported in whole or in part or in any manner or form without the prior written consent of Scholastic Ltd. Any such unauthorised use or activities are prohibited and may give rise to civil liabilities and criminal prosecutions.

The material contained on this CD-ROM may only be used in the context for which it was intended in *Read & Respond,* and is for use only by the purchaser or purchasing institution that has purchased the book and CD-ROM. Permission to download images is given for purchasers only and not for users from any lending service. Any further use of the material contravenes Scholastic Ltd's copyright and that of other rights holders.

This CD-ROM has been tested for viruses at all stages of its production. However, we recommend that you run virus-checking software on your computer systems at all times. Scholastic Ltd cannot accept any responsibility for any loss, disruption or damage to your data or your computer system that may occur as a result of using either the CD-ROM or the data held on it.

IF YOU ACCEPT THE ABOVE CONDITIONS YOU MAY PROCEED TO USE THE CD-ROM.

Recommended system requirements:
Windows: XP (Service Pack 3), Vista (Service Pack 2), Windows 7 or Windows 8 with 2.33GHz processor
Mac: OS 10.6 to 10.8 with Intel Core™ Duo processor
1GB RAM (recommended)
1024 x 768 Screen resolution
CD-ROM drive (24x speed recommended)
Adobe Reader (version 9 recommended for Mac users)
Broadband internet connections (for installation and updates)

For all technical support queries (including no CD drive), please phone Scholastic Customer Services on 0845 6039091.

Designed using Adobe Indesign
Scholastic Education, an imprint of Scholastic Ltd
Book End, Range Road, Witney, Oxfordshire, OX29 0YD
Registered office: Westfield Road, Southam, Warwickshire CV47 0RA

Printed and bound by Ashford Colour Press
© 2016 Scholastic Ltd
2 3 4 5 6 7 8 9   8 9 0 1 2 3 4 5

British Library Cataloguing-in-Publication Data
A catalogue record for this book is available from the British Library.
ISBN 978-14071-6057-3

Extracts from *The National Curriculum in England, English Programme of Study* © Crown Copyright. Reproduced under the terms of the Open Government Licence (OGL). http://www.nationalarchives.gov.uk/doc/open-government-licence/version/3

Due to the nature of the web, we cannot guarantee the content or links of any site mentioned. We strongly recommend that teachers check websites before using them in the classroom.

Author Helen Lewis
Editorial team Rachel Morgan, Jenny Wilcox, Vicki Yates, Elizabeth Evans
Series designer Neil Salt
Design team Anna Oliwa
Illustrator Mike Lacey
Photo Image of Michelle Magorian; Credit Shaun Curry / Stringer @ Getty Images
Digital development Hannah Barnett, Phil Crothers and MWA Technologies Private Ltd

Acknowledgements
The publishers gratefully acknowledge permission to reproduce the following copyright material:

Penguin Random House UK for the use of the cover and extract text from *Goodnight Mister Tom* written by Michelle Magiorian (Puffin, 2010). Copyright © Michelle Magiorian, 1981.

Every effort has been made to trace copyright holders for the works reproduced in this book, and the publishers apologise for any inadvertent omissions.

CONTENTS

INTRODUCTION

Read & Respond provides teaching ideas related to a specific children's book. The series focuses on best-loved books and brings you ways to use them to engage your class and enthuse them about reading.

The book is divided into different sections:

- **About the book and author:** gives you some background information about the book and the author.

- **Guided reading:** breaks the book down into sections and gives notes for using it with guided reading groups. A bookmark has been provided on page 12 containing comprehension questions. The children can be directed to refer to these as they read.

- **Shared reading:** provides extracts from the children's books with associated notes for focused work. There is also one non-fiction extract that relates to the children's book.

- **Grammar, punctuation & spelling:** provides word-level work related to the children's book so you can teach grammar, punctuation and spelling in context.

- **Plot, character & setting:** contains activity ideas focused on the plot, characters and the setting of the story.

- **Talk about it:** has speaking and listening activities related to the children's book. These activities may be based directly on the children's book or be broadly based on the themes and concepts of the story.

- **Get writing:** provides writing activities related to the children's book. These activities may be based directly on the children's book or be broadly based on the themes and concepts of the story.

- **Assessment:** contains short activities that will help you assess whether the children have understood concepts and curriculum objectives. They are designed to be informal activities to feed into your planning.

The activities follow the same format:

- **Objective:** the objective for the lesson. It will be based upon a curriculum objective, but will often be more specific to the focus being covered.

- **What you need:** a list of resources you need to teach the lesson, including digital resources (printable pages, interactive activities and media resources, see page 5).

- **What to do:** the activity notes.

- **Differentiation:** this is provided where specific and useful differentiation advice can be given to support and/or extend the learning in the activity. Differentiation by providing additional adult support has not been included as this will be at a teacher's discretion based upon specific children's needs and ability, as well as the availability of support.

The activities are numbered for reference within each section and should move through the text sequentially – so you can use the lesson while you are reading the book. Once you have read the book, most of the activities can be used in any order you wish.

Below are brief guidance notes for using the CD-ROM. For more detailed information, please click on the '?' button in the top right-hand corner of the screen.

The program contains the following:

- the extract pages from the book
- all of the photocopiable pages from the book
- additional printable pages
- interactive on-screen activities
- media resources.

Getting started

Put the CD-ROM into your CD-ROM drive. If you do not have a CD-ROM drive, phone Scholastic Customer Services on 0845 6039091.

- For Windows users, the install wizard should autorun, if it fails to do so then navigate to your CD-ROM drive. Then follow the installation process.
- For Mac users, copy the disk image file to your hard drive. After it has finished copying double click it to mount the disk image. Navigate to the mounted disk image and run the installer. After installation the disk image can be unmounted and the DMG can be deleted from the hard drive.
- To install on a network, see the ReadMe file located on the CD-ROM (navigate to your drive).

To complete the installation of the program you need to open the program and click 'Update' in the pop-up. Please note – this CD-ROM is web-enabled and the content will be downloaded from the internet to your hard drive to populate the CD-ROM with the relevant resources. This only needs to be done on first use, after this you will be able to use the CD-ROM without an internet connection. If at any point any content is updated, you will receive another pop-up upon start up when there is an internet connection.

Main menu

The main menu is the first screen that appears. Here you can access: terms and conditions, registration links, how to use the CD-ROM and credits. To access a specific book click on the relevant button (NB only titles installed will be available). You can filter by the

drop-down lists if you wish. You can search all resources by clicking 'Search' in the bottom left-hand corner. You can also log in and access favourites that you have bookmarked.

Resources

By clicking on a book on the Main menu, you are taken to the resources for that title. The resources are: Media, Interactives, Extracts and Printables. Select the category and then launch a resource by clicking the play button.

Teacher settings

In the top right-hand corner of the screen is a small 'T' icon. This is the teacher settings area. It is password protected, the password is: login. This area will allow you to choose the print quality settings for interactive activities ('Default' or 'Best') and also allow you to check for updates to the program or re-download all content to the disk via Refresh all content. You can also set up user logins so that you can save and access favourites. Once a user is set up, they can enter by clicking the login link underneath the 'T' and '?' buttons.

Search

You can access an all resources search by clicking the search button on the bottom left of the Main menu. You can search for activities by type (using the drop-down filter) or by keyword by typing into the box. You can then assign resources to your favourites area or launch them directly from the search area.

CURRICULUM LINKS

Section	Activity	Curriculum objectives
Guided reading		Comprehension: To maintain positive attitudes to reading and understanding of what they read.
Shared reading	1	Comprehension: To draw inferences about characters' feelings, thoughts and motives.
	2	Comprehension: To discuss and evaluate how authors use language, considering the impact on the reader.
	3	Comprehension: To make comparisons within and across books.
	4	Comprehension: To explore the meaning of words in context.
Grammar, punctuation & spelling	1	Composition: To use modal verbs or adverbs to indicate degrees of possibility.
	2	Transcription: To spell words ending in 'able', 'ible', 'ably' and 'ibly'.
	3	Composition: To use semi-colons, colons or dashes to mark the boundary between independent clauses.
	4	Transcription: To distinguish between homophones and other words which are often confused.
	5	Composition: To use passive verbs to affect the presentation of information in a sentence.
	6	Transcription: To use a thesaurus.
Plot, character & setting	1	Comprehension: To maintain positive attitudes to reading and understand what they read.
	2	Composition: To précis longer passages.
	3	Composition: To assess the effectiveness of their own and others' writing.
	4	Comprehension: To draw inferences such as inferring characters' feelings, thoughts and motives from their actions, and justifying inferences with evidence.
	5	Comprehension: To identify and discuss themes and conventions in and across a wide range of writing.
	6	Comprehension: To discuss and evaluate how authors use language, including figurative language, considering the impact on the reader.
	7	Comprehension: To make comparisons within and across books.
	8	Comprehension: To identify and discuss themes and conventions in and across a wide range of writing.

Section	Activity	Curriculum objectives
Talk about it	1	Spoken language: To give well-structured descriptions and explanations for different purposes, including for expressing feelings.
	2	Spoken language: To use spoken language to develop understanding through hypothesising, imagining and exploring ideas.
	3	Spoken language: To participate in role play and improvisation.
	4	Spoken language: To participate in presentations, speaking audibly and fluently.
	5	Spoken language: To ask relevant questions to extend their understanding and knowledge.
	6	Spoken language: To give well-structured narratives.
Get writing	1	Composition: To plan writing by identifying the audience and purpose of the writing.
	2	Composition: To ensure the consistent and correct use of tense throughout a piece of writing.
	3	Composition: To use a wide range of devices to build cohesion within and across paragraphs.
	4	Composition: To proofread for spelling and punctuation errors.
	5	Composition: To select grammar and vocabulary to enhance meaning.
	6	Composition: To perform their own compositions with appropriate intonation, volume and movement so that meaning is clear.
Assessment	1	Comprehension: To participate in discussion about books they have read.
	2	Composition: To propose changes to vocabulary, grammar and punctuation to enhance effects and clarify meaning.
	3	Comprehension: To recommend books they have read to their peers, giving reasons for their choices.
	4	Comprehension: To draw inferences such as inferring characters' feelings, thoughts and motives from their actions, and justifying inferences with evidence.
	5	Comprehension: To explain and discuss their understanding of what they have read through formal debate.
	6	Comprehension: To ask relevant questions to improve their understanding.

GOODNIGHT MISTER TOM

About the book

Ever since it was first published in 1981, *Goodnight Mister Tom* has been hailed as a modern classic. Set against the backdrop of the early days of World War II, it's a powerful and touching story about human relationships and the healing power of love.

In September 1939, William Beech, a timid and malnourished child from London, is evacuated to the countryside. He's billeted with the elderly Tom Oakley, a reclusive widower. Behind his gruff exterior, Mister Tom, as William calls him, is a kind and gentle man, and William begins to flourish under his care. But then William's abusive mother calls him back home.

After having a premonition that William is in trouble, Tom goes to London to look for him. He finds him beaten, chained, abandoned and clutching his dead baby sister. After a brief stay in hospital, during which the authorities decide to send William to a children's home, Tom kidnaps him and takes him back home.

William has barely recovered from his ordeal before his best friend Zach is killed in an air raid while visiting his parents. William is overcome with grief, but gradually learns to accept Zach's death. He realises he has a lot to live for and appreciates the happiness he has found in his new life with Tom.

Goodnight Mister Tom has been adapted multiple times: for radio, theatre (as both a play and a musical) and, in 1998, as a TV film starring the late John Thaw. The television adaptation won seven television awards, including a BAFTA.

About the author

Michelle Magorian was born in Portsmouth in 1947. As a child, her ambition was to become an actress. After leaving school, she trained for three years at the Rose Bruford College of Speech and Drama and for a further two years at Marcel Marceau's mime school in Paris.

Michelle began her acting career working in repertory companies and spent several years touring the UK. It was during this time that she developed a particular interest in children's books and decided to write one herself. The result was *Goodnight Mister Tom*, published in 1981.

Since then, Michelle has divided her time between acting and writing. She has acted in theatre, television and film. She has also toured England and Italy with her one-woman mime show. To date she has had seven novels published, including *Back Home*, another story about a child evacuated during World War II, and *Just Henry*, which won the Costa Book Award in 2008.

Key facts

Goodnight Mister Tom

Author: Michelle Magorian

First published: 1981 by Kestrel Books

Awards: The book has won numerous awards around the world, including The Guardian Children's Fiction Prize and the International Reading Award.

Did you know? *Goodnight Mister Tom* took Michelle four and a half years to write, as she had to fit it in between acting jobs.

First impressions

Before you begin reading the story, spend time talking with the children about the cover and blurb of the book. Encourage them to look closely at the cover to find out everything they can about the book from it. Although covers may vary, they all contain similar information and all want to grab the potential reader's attention and entice them in. Ask: *What can you tell about the story just by looking at the front cover? What clues does the illustration give you about the characters and setting of the story? What do you think the story might be about?*

Turn over the book and look at the back cover. Ask: *Does reading the blurb confirm any of the deductions you made when you looked at the front cover? Does the blurb give you any extra information?*

....

Getting started (Chapter 1)

Before beginning to read the book, establish that the story begins in September 1939, at the start of World War II. Discuss the evacuation of children during the war. The woman who brings Willie to Tom's house describes herself as a billeting officer. Explain that billeting officers were volunteers who took on the job of finding homes for evacuees. You could display and discuss the media resource 'Children being evacuated'.

Read the first chapter together. Organise the children into pairs to discuss (and possibly make notes on) question 1 on the Guided Reading Bookmark (page 12). Ask a volunteer to share their summary with the class.

Ask: *What do you learn about Willie from the first chapter?* (He's pale and thin; he feels frightened and lonely; he has limp sandy hair and dull grey eyes; he has bruises and sores on his legs; he's from a poor family (bacon was a luxury for lodgers or visitors); he thinks he's bad (his mum has told him so); his mother beats him; he's polite (probably due to fear); he normally dreads school; he's frightened of lots of things; he expects to get into trouble.)

Ask: *What do you learn about Tom from the first chapter?* (He's old; he's strong and healthy; he's got white hair; he is average height; he can be abrupt when he talks to people, but he's kind.) Ask: *What things does Tom do that show his kindness?* (He shows his kindness in the way he acts towards Willie; for example, offering to put up a peg at the right height for him; giving him a good meal; giving him a scarf when he sees he is cold; not speaking harshly to him when he threatens to kill Sammy; tucking a blanket around him. Tom also shows his kindness in the way he talks to Sammy.)

Together, discuss question 2 from the Bookmark.

....

Settling in (Chapters 2–5)

Read Chapters 2 to 5 together. Ask: *What further evidence is there in these chapters that Willie comes from a deprived background?* (The contents of his suitcase; he's never toasted bread before; he's never eaten cake before; he sleeps under the bed instead of in it; he's malnourished; he's astonished when Tom buys him a sweet and a comic.)

Briefly discuss the events leading up to the outbreak of World War II. On 1 September 1939 Germany invaded Poland. Britain immediately issued ultimatum was ignored and two days later Britain declared war on Germany. Discuss the scene in Chapter 5, in which the church congregation listens to war being declared on the wireless. Ask: *Do you think it would have been normal for people to listen to the radio in church? Why do you think they did it on this occasion? What other clues in the story show that people knew war was coming?*

Explain that Anderson shelters were a type of air-raid shelter designed to accommodate up to six people. They were made of corrugated steel panels and buried in the ground. You could display the media resource 'Anderson shelter'. At the end of Chapter 5 Willie gets hot when he's digging the trench for the Anderson shelter. Ask: *Why won't he take his sweater off?*

Discuss question 3 from the Guided Reading Bookmark.

On the road to recovery (Chapters 6–11)

Read Chapters 6 to 11 together. Ask: *How would you describe Zach?* (confident, friendly, talkative, enthusiastic, exuberant) *How does the author communicate Zach's character?* (through what Zach says and how he says it; through what Zach does and how he does it; also through description of what Zach looks like)

Ask: *How does the outbreak of war affect Tom's behaviour?* (He goes to a village meeting and volunteers to help out; before he kept himself to himself.) *Why do you think Tom's behaviour changes?* (Partly through a sense of duty because it is wartime and partly through an increased sense of responsibility now he has a child to look after.)

Ask: *What events in these chapters help Willie start to feel better about himself?* (Zach saying he likes Willie; making blackberry jam; Willie's friends

coming round to commiserate with him about being in a class with younger children; gifts on his birthday; drawing; a surprise party)

Ask: *By the end of these chapters, how can you tell that Willie is on the road to recovery?* (He has his first night when he doesn't wet the bed; there is only one sore left on his arm and it's nearly healed.) Discuss questions 4, 10, 11 and 12 from the Guided Reading Bookmark.

Changes (Chapters 12-14)

Read Chapters 12 to 14 together. Ask: *How do events in the wider world affect life in Little Weirwold?* (The failure of the anticipated bombing raids to materialise leads to evacuees being called back home and the Christmas play having to be recast. Because Mr Bush has been called up, Tom takes over the choir. George's brother Michael is reported missing, presumed dead.)

Chapter 14 contains a description of Mrs Hartridge's classroom and a whole day's worth of lessons. Ask children to discuss the differences between modern classrooms and lessons and those of 1939. You could display and discuss the media resource '1930s classrooms'.

At the end of Chapter 14 Tom receives a letter from Willie's mother saying she's ill and wants Willie to go back home for a while. Discuss question 5 from the Guided Reading Bookmark.

Back home (Chapters 15–17)

Read Chapters 15 to 17 together. There are some very disturbing scenes at the end of Chapter 15 and at the beginning of Chapter 17. You may want to familiarise yourself with the content of these before approaching them with the children.

After reading Chapter 15 ask: *The way Willie's*

mother treats him and the baby is shocking. But do you find it surprising? Explain your answer.

Ask: *What makes Willie's suffering at the hands of his mother even worse than it used to be before he was evacuated?* (The fact that he now realises the way his mother treats him is not normal; He now knows what it means to be loved.)

After reading Chapter 17 ask: *Why does Tom decide to kidnap Will? What do you think might happen later as a result of this decision?*

Discuss questions 6, 7, 8 and 13 from the Guided Reading Bookmark.

Happiness and tragedy (Chapters 18–21)

Read Chapters 18 to 21 together. After reading Chapter 18, ask: *How does Zach upset Will?* (by mentioning babies) *Why do you think this upsets Will?* (because it reminds him of Trudy) *How does Will get over his feelings of guilt over the death of Trudy?* (by interacting with Mrs Hartridge's baby)

After reading Chapter 20, ask: *What does Will's reaction to the woman from the children's home tell you about how he has changed since the beginning of the story?* (The fact that Will is prepared to stand up for himself and Tom shows how much he's grown in confidence. He is no longer timid and fearful, as he was at the beginning of the story.)

After reading Chapter 21, ask children to look back at Chapter 19, in which Tom, Will and Zach go on holiday to the seaside. Ask: *What is the purpose of Chapter 19?* (To paint a picture of an idyllic way of life that will soon be destroyed by the war and to

make Zach's death seem even more of a tragedy by contrasting it with the happiness of the holiday.) You could watch the media resource 'The Blitz'.

Learning to live again (Chapters 22–23)

Read Chapters 22 and 23 together. After reading Chapter 22 ask: *How does Will's behaviour change after Zach's death?* (He can't enjoy anything.) *Why?* (He feels numb from grief.) *Which events help Will adjust to life without Zach?* (drawing a picture of a photograph of Geoffrey and his best friend who was killed; listening to the same music Geoffrey was playing the day he and Zach first went to Spooky Cott; whacking a dead branch against a tree; riding Zach's bike) *How do these events help him?* (They help him to get in touch with Zach in his imagination; They help him express his anger at Zach's death.)

Ask: *Why do you think the author chose to 'kill off' Zach?* (So that Will has a reason to take on aspects of Zach's personality that will help him grow and change in the ways he needs to in order to become whole and happy.)

Discuss questions 15 to 18 from the Guided Reading Bookmark.

Second reading

Use a second reading of the novel to explore key features of the story in more depth. Use questions 9, 14 and 19 from the Guided Reading Bookmark to help focus discussions.

SCHOLASTIC
READ&RESPOND
Bringing the best books to life in the classroom

Goodnight Mister Tom
by Michelle Magorian

Focus on...
Meaning

1. Summarise the first chapter.

2. What themes does the first chapter introduce? How might they be explored in the rest of the book?

3. What do the names of the characters suggest about them?

4. Why do Willie and Zach like each other? Give evidence from what you have read.

5. Predict what might happen next. Give evidence from what you have read so far.

Focus on...
Organisation

6. How do the chapter titles add to the story?

7. Suggest an alternative title for a chapter that you have read.

8. Choose a chapter that you have read. What devices does the author use to build tension and anticipation?

9. The story is told in chronological order. Why do you think the author chose to organise the story in this way?

SCHOLASTIC
READ&RESPOND
Bringing the best books to life in the classroom

Goodnight Mister Tom
by Michelle Magorian

Focus on...
Language and features

10. Why do you think the author wrote much of the dialogue in non-standard English?

11. What can you tell about Willie from the way he talks?

12. How is the way Zach talks different from the way Willie talks? What does that tell you?

13. At the end of Chapter 15, Willie begins calling himself Will. What is the significance of this?

14. How does the wartime setting add to the story?

Focus on...
Purpose, viewpoints and effects

15. Who is your favourite character? Why?

16. Which part of the story do you find the most moving? Why?

17. How does William benefit from his relationship with Tom and vice versa?

18. In what ways does William change over the course of the story? What causes this?

19. What do you think the book's important message is?

Extract 1

- Display an enlarged copy of Extract 1. Read the extract together. Ask: *What emotion does Sammy trigger in Willie?* (fear) Ask: *Why do you think Willie is scared of Sammy?* (he's not used to dogs; his mother has told him dogs spread deadly diseases; he's scared of everything; Sammy's boisterous behaviour)

- Give out individuals or pairs copies of the extract and ask children to underline all the parts of the text that show Willie is afraid.

- Establish that the author expresses Willie's fear in various ways: directly (for example, Willie was more petrified of the dog than he had been of the squirrel); through Willie's actions (for example, Willie let out a shriek and drew back); through Willie's words (for example, 'I'll kill you.'); through Willie's bodily sensations (for example, sweat broke out from under his armpits and across his forehead).

- Re-read paragraph 2 together. Establish that remembering the tiny children's graves prompts Willie to pick up the branch. Ask: *What do you think Willie is thinking at this point?* (That the children whose graves he saw might have died from being bitten by dogs.) *What does that tell you about Willie?* (He doesn't know much about dogs, animals or the world in general and that he believes what his mother tells him.) *Why does Willie pick up the branch?* (To defend himself against the dog because he thinks it's attacking him.)

- This scene is written from Willie's perspective. Ask children to imagine the same scene written from Tom or Sammy's perspective. How would it be different?

Extract 2

- Display an enlarged copy of Extract 2 and read it together.

- Draw children's attention to the description of Willie (the text in the first paragraph that isn't dialogue). Ask them to underline the adjectives used to describe Willie and what he's wearing. Encourage children to use one colour for adjectives describing what Willie used to look like and another colour for adjectives describing what he looks like now.

- Encouraging children to refer to the adjectives they've underlined, ask: *How does the author emphasise how much Willie has changed?* (by using contrasting adjectives: 'thick' and 'sturdy' to contrast with 'thin', 'upright' to contrast with 'little', and the colours 'green', 'navy-blue' and 'pink' to contrast with 'grey')

- Ask: *How does the author suggest Willie is healthy?* (He is described as 'well-fleshed', his hair as 'shiny', his forehead and cheeks as 'round and pink'.) Establish that Willie's health contrasts with that of his mother. Draw children's attention to the description of Willie's mother's face in the third paragraph from the end. Ask: *How does the author suggest Willie's mother is ill? What effect does this have on the reader?* (It draws out sympathy for Willie's mother.)

- Ask: *How does Willie's mother's clothing contrast with the clothes she sent Willie away in when he was evacuated?* (The shoes she's wearing are described as 'smart' but the clothes she sent Willie away in were thin and shabby.) *What does this contrast suggest about Willie's mother?* (She pays more attention to her own clothes than she does to Willie's.) *What effect does this have on the reader?* (It makes you less sympathetic towards Willie's mother.)

Extract 3

- Display an enlarged copy of Extract 3 and also give out individual copies.

- Choose five volunteers to read the extract aloud with expression (a narrator and the four characters).

- Ask: *What evidence is there in this extract that Will and his mother didn't have a good relationship?* (For Will, his mother wanting him back would be bad news; he smiles with relief when he finds out she doesn't want him back; he doesn't show grief at the news of his mother's death.)

- Ask children to work in pairs and discuss the evidence in the extract that shows Will has changed since the beginning of the book. Before children do this, you might like to give them an opportunity to re-read Extract 1, to remind them what Willie was like when he first arrived at Tom's.

- Discuss the evidence children have found that shows Will has changed (for example, he answers adults when they talk to him; he's happy, unable to understand why someone would commit suicide and thinking about all the things there are to live for; he looks the woman straight in the eye; he stands up for himself; he defends Tom).

- Ask: *What evidence is there in Extract 3 that Will is not completely fearless?* (He says 'No' and he takes a deep breath before saying he wasn't kidnapped, but rescued.) *Why do you think the author shows us that Will is still afraid?* (To emphasise his bravery – he's scared, but he stands up for himself and Tom anyway.)

Extract 4

- Read together an enlarged copy of Extract 4. Discuss the genre and style of writing and compare it to the previous extracts. Ask: *Is this text fiction or non-fiction? Descriptive or informative? Does it have facts, opinions or both?*

- Consider the text organisation. Number the paragraphs. Ask: *Would it make a difference if the text were all in one paragraph?* (The short paragraphs make it clearer and more readable.)

- Underline the phrase 'the infirm' in paragraph 1. Ask: *What does this phrase mean in this context?* (For example, people who are unwell or in poor health.)

- Ask children to locate the word 'evacuees' in paragraph 2. Ask: *What part of speech is 'evacuees'?* (a noun) *What verb is 'evacuees' formed from?* (to evacuate) *What does 'evacuees' mean?* (people who were evacuated – in other words, moved away from their home to a safer place) Ask children to suggest other nouns that are formed in the same way as 'evacuee' and give the verb they are formed from (for example, 'interviewee' from 'to interview'; 'employee' from 'to employ'; 'addressee' from 'to address'; 'trainee' from 'to train'; 'licensee' from 'to license').

- Ask children to locate the phrase 'had failed to materialise' in paragraph 6. Ask: *What other phrase could replace it without changing the meaning of the sentence?* (For example, hadn't happened.)

- Re-read paragraph 7. Ask: *What was the Blitz?* (you might want to show them media resource 'The Blitz') *What were the V-1 and V-2 attacks?* If you have studied World War II in history lessons, children may be able to answer these questions. If not, ask children to use their skills of inference to suggest what they might be. You could ask them to find out for themselves later.

Extract 1

Chapter 1

A small black-and-white collie ran around the tree and into the leaves. It stopped in front of him and jumped up into the air. Willie was more petrified of the dog than he had been of the squirrel.

'Them poisonous dogs,' he heard his mother's voice saying inside him. 'One bite from them mutts and you're dead. They got 'orrible diseases in 'em.' He remembered the tiny children's graves and quickly picked up a thick branch from the ground.

'You go away,' he said feebly, gripping it firmly in his hand. 'You go away.'

The dog sprang into the air again and barked and yapped at him, tossing leaves by his legs. Willie let out a shriek and drew back. The dog came nearer.

'I'll kill you.'

'I wouldn't do that,' said a deep voice behind him. He turned to find Tom standing by the outer branches. 'He ent goin' to do you no 'arm, so I should jest drop that if I was you.'

Willie froze with the branch still held high in his hand. Sweat broke out from under his armpits and across his forehead. Now he was for it. He was bound to get a beating now. Tom came towards him, took the branch firmly from his hand and lifted it up. Willie automatically flung his arm across his face and gave a cry but the blow he was expecting never came. Tom had merely thrown the branch to the other end of the graveyard and the dog had gone scampering after it.

'You can take yer arm down now, boy,' he said quietly. 'I think you and I 'ad better go inside and sort a few things out. Come on,' and with that he stepped aside for Willie to go in front of him along the path.

Extract 2

Chapter 15

'Mum!' he cried. 'Mum!'

'Go away,' she said sternly. 'You won't get no money from me.'

'Mum,' he repeated, 'it's me.'

She glanced down and was about to tell him to clear off when she recognized him. Yes. It was Willie but he had altered so much. She had been looking for a thin little boy dressed in grey. Here stood an upright, well-fleshed boy in sturdy ankle boots, thick woollen socks, a green rolled-top jersey, and a navy-blue coat and balaclava. His hair stuck out in a shiny mass above his forehead and his cheeks were round and pink. It was a great shock to her.

'I'm awfully pleased to see you, Mum. I've such a lot to tell you and there's me pictures, like.'

She was startled at his peculiar mixture of accents. She had expected him to be more subservient but even his voice sounded louder.

'I'm sorry,' she said. 'I'm not very well, you see, and I'm a bit tired. I wasn't expectin' such a change in you.'

Willie was puzzled.

He thought that it was his mother that had changed. He had learnt new things, that was true, but he was still him.

He studied her face. She was very pale, almost yellow in colour and her lips were so blue that it seemed as if every ounce of blood had been drained from them. The lines by her thin mouth curved downwards. He glanced at her body. She was wearing a long black coat, fawn stockings and smart lace-up heeled shoes. A small shopping bag was now leaning against her leg.

He touched her arm gently.

'I'll carry that for you, Mum,' he said, picking it up. She spun round and gave his hand a sharp slap.

Extract 3

Chapter 20

'I'm afraid we've brought you some rather bad news, William,' she said. 'It concerns your mother.'

He looked at her, startled.

'She wants me back?'

'No.'

He smiled with relief. She paused.

'William,' she hesitated. 'I'm afraid your mother is dead. She committed suicide.'

He looked blankly at her.

'I don't get you.'

'She killed herself.'

Will gazed at her in stunned disbelief.

'Killed herself? But...but why?'

'I don't know. I suppose she just didn't want to live any more.'

How could anyone not want to live, thought Will, when there were so many things to live for? There were rainy nights and wind and the slap of the sea and the moon. There were books to read and pictures to paint and music.

'I'm from a Children's Home in Sussex,' she explained. 'It's an orphanage and it's right out in the country. There are lots of children there and we usually find foster parents to take them into their homes, young parents with children of their own.' And she smiled.

'What the lady is saying,' said the policeman, 'is that she's willin' to have you at the Home.'

Will thrust his hands deep into his pockets and looked her straight in the eye.

'No,' he said, somewhat shakily, 'I'm not willin'. This is my home and I'm stayin' here.'

'Now now, son,' said the warden. 'That ain't the way to talk. You don't have much choice in the matter. Your Mr Oakley has not bin keepin' to the lor. Kidnappin's a serious offence.'

Will took a deep breath.

'When you kidnap someone you usually want a ransom. There ent no one in the world who'd pay a ransom for me,' and he glanced at Tom, 'except Mister Tom perhaps and he's the one that's supposed to have kidnapped me. Well, I reckon I weren't kidnapped. I reckon I was rescued.'

Extract 4

Fear that German bombing would cause civilian deaths prompted the government to evacuate children, mothers with babies and the infirm from British towns and cities during World War II.

Evacuation took place in several waves. The first wave came on 1 September 1939 – the day Germany invaded Poland and two days before the British declaration of war. Over the course of three days, one and a half million evacuees were sent to rural locations considered to be safe.

Evacuation required thousands of volunteer helpers, including teachers, local authority officials, railway staff and 17,000 members of the Women's Voluntary Service (WVS). Volunteers were also needed to host evacuees.

Parents were issued with a list detailing what their children should take with them. These items included a gas mask, a change of underclothes, nightclothes, plimsolls (or slippers), spare stockings or socks, a toothbrush, a comb, a towel, soap, a face cloth, handkerchiefs and a warm coat. Many families struggled to provide their children with all of the items on the list.

Evacuees and their hosts were often astonished to see how each other lived. Some evacuees flourished in their new surroundings. Others endured a miserable time away from home. Many evacuees from inner-city areas had never seen farm animals before or eaten vegetables.

By the end of 1939, the widely expected bombing raids on cities had failed to materialise, so many parents whose children had been evacuated in September decided to bring them home again.

More rounds of evacuation took place in the summer and autumn of 1940, following the German invasion of France and the beginning of the Blitz, and in 1944, following the V-1 and V-2 attacks.

For some children, the end of the war brought an end to a prolonged period of fear, confusion and separation. For others, it brought considerable upheaval as they returned to cities and families they barely remembered.

GRAMMAR, PUNCTUATION & SPELLING

1. Likely language

Objective
To use adverbials or modal verbs to indicate degrees of possibility.

What you need
Copies of *Goodnight Mister Tom*, plain paper, photocopiable page 22 'Likely language'.

What to do
- Recap the events in the latest chapter of *Goodnight Mister Tom* you've read in class. Ask: *What do you think will happen next?*

- Divide children into groups, asking them to come up with four suggestions of what will happen next, writing each on a separate piece of paper, using the word 'will', for example, 'Willie will get stronger'.

- On the board draw a horizontal probability line, labelling the left end 'impossible' and the right end 'certain'. Ask each group to use the concept of the probability line to order their written suggestions in terms of how likely they are. Challenge groups to write two more suggestions: one impossible and one certain.

- Explain that when speaking or writing, we can't use a probability line to indicate possibility so we need to use language instead. Give out and discuss copies of photocopiable page 22 'Likely language'.

- Ask children to use the language on the photocopiable sheet to rewrite each of their suggestions to show how likely they think it is.

Differentiation
Support: Revise using comparative adjectives to compare the likelihood of two or more events. For example, likely, less likely, least likely; probable, more probable, most probable.
Extension: Invite children to write suggestions about unknown events in the past. For example, you could ask them to suggest why Tom went to live in the cottage next to the church.

2. Sensible suffixes

Objective
To spell words ending in 'able', 'ible', 'ably' and 'ibly'.

What you need
Photocopiable page 23 'Sensible suffixes'.

What to do
- Ask: *What is a suffix?* Discuss the meaning of the suffixes 'able' and 'ible' (capable of being). For example, the adjective 'enjoyable' means capable of being enjoyed. Discuss the related adverbial endings 'ably' and 'ibly'.

- The endings 'able' and 'ably':
  - are used if there is a related word ending in 'ation' (for example, applicable)
  - are usually used if a complete root word can be heard before them, even if there is no related word ending in 'ation' (for example, suitable)
  - if added to a word ending in 'ce' or 'ge', the 'e' must be kept, in order to keep the sound of the 'c' or 'g' soft (for example, serviceable, changeable).

- The endings 'ible' and 'ibly':
  - are usually used when a complete root word cannot be heard before them (for example horrible). However, there are a few exceptions (most notably, sensible).

- Give out copies of photocopiable page 23 'Sensible suffixes'. Ask the children to use the listed rules to select the correct spelling of each word in bold.

Differentiation
Support: In the second bullet-pointed activity on the photocopiable sheet, ask children to write sentences of their own around only a few of the adverbs rather than all eight of them.
Extension: Challenge children to list as many 'able' and 'ible' adjectives as they can, then check each other's spellings using a dictionary.

3. Classy clauses

Objective

To use semi-colons, colons or dashes to mark the boundary between independent clauses.

What you need

Photocopiable page 24 'Classy clauses', scissors.

What to do

- Revise the term 'independent clause' (a clause that can stand by itself as a sentence). On the board write two related independent clauses, for example:
  - A: Zach offered to show Willie around
  - B: he'd already been there for a week

- Explain that we can use a semi-colon or a dash to join two related independent clauses together to form a single sentence. Ask children to join the two clauses on the board in this way. For example: Zach offered to show Willie around; he'd already been there for a week.

- Repeat the activity using pairs of independent clauses suggested by the children.

- Explain that sometimes we can use a colon to join two independent clauses (when the second clause explains the information given in the first, or provides more detail about it). For example, 'Tom could tell Willie got beaten at home: he had bruises all over him.' Tell children if they aren't sure which punctuation to use, to use a semi-colon or a dash.

- Give out photocopiable page 24 'Classy clauses', asking children to complete it independently.

Differentiation

Support: Provide children with more pairs of independent clauses to match up and join together.
Extension: Ask children to devise their own version of the activity on the photocopiable sheet and give it to a friend to complete.

4. No more confusion

Objective

To distinguish between homophones.

What you need

Interactive activity 'Which word?', dictionaries, computers (optional), card, scissors.

What to do

- Revise the term 'homophones' (words that sound the same but are spelled differently and have different meanings). Ask children to give a few examples.

- Ask pairs to list as many groups of homophones as they can within a given time. You could challenge children to find a certain number of homophone groups, depending on their ability.

- Ask children to write groups of homophones on the board, explain their meanings, and share any mnemonics they may use to help distinguish between them (for example, 'here' and 'hear': you hear with your ear).

- Introduce the interactive activity 'Which word?'. You might want to play the game with the whole class (maybe dividing children into mixed-ability groups). Alternatively, pairs or groups could play the game on computers or tablets. Either way, encourage children to use a dictionary to check word meanings.

- End the lesson with a spelling quiz. Read out sentences containing homophones covered during the lesson and ask children (working individually or in pairs) to write the words as they should be spelled in each sentence.

Differentiation

Support: Ask children to create a simple card game in which homophones need to be matched to their meanings. Get pairs to swap work and match each other's cards.
Extension: Ask children to write their own homophone sentences based on *Goodnight Mister Tom*, using a similar format to the interactive activity. Get pairs to swap work and complete each other's sentences.

5. Passive puzzle

Objective

To use passive verbs to affect the presentation of information in a sentence.

What you need

Printable page 'Forming the passive voice', interactive activity 'Passive puzzle', copies of *Goodnight Mister Tom*, computers.

What to do

- On the board write two similar sentences, one in the active voice and one in the passive voice; for example:
  - The Germans bombed London.
  - London was bombed by the Germans.

- Remind children that verbs can be active or passive. In the active voice, the subject performs the action. In the passive voice, the subject is acted upon by someone or something else.

- Discuss the difference in emphasis between the two sentences: the active version emphasises the doer (the Germans), whereas the passive version emphasises the thing acted upon (London). Emphasise this by rubbing out 'by the Germans'.

- Explain that the passive voice is used to draw attention to the person or thing acted upon and/ or when the doer of the action is not important (for example, Tom was seen leaving the hospital). It can also be used to deflect unwanted attention; for example, 'The window has been broken' rather than 'I have broken the window'.

- Display and discuss an enlarged copy of printable page 'Forming the passive voice'.

- Introduce the interactive activity 'Passive puzzle'. Allow time for pairs to complete the activity. Display the printable sheet for reference.

Differentiation

Support: During the interactive activity, pair less confident learners with a more confident partner.
Extension: Ask children to choose several active sentences from *Goodnight Mister Tom* and rewrite them in the passive voice.

6. Vocabulary upgrade

Objective

To use a thesaurus.

What you need

Printable page 'Vocabulary upgrade', thesauruses, copies of *Goodnight Mister Tom*.

What to do

- On the board write a sentence containing the verb 'walk' (for example: Zach walked across the stage). Ask children to suggest an alternative word to replace 'walked'.

- Ask: *If you were writing this sentence, would you choose 'walked', or one of the alternatives? Why?* ('Walked' is overused, making it less interesting; the other verbs are more specific; they give you a clearer picture of what is happening.)

- Revise the term 'synonym'. Challenge children, working in pairs, to find as many synonyms as they can for another overused word (for example, 'said') in a given time limit (say, two minutes).

- Give out the thesauruses. If necessary, revise how to use a thesaurus.

- Write a sentence on the board using the verb 'like'; for example: Willie likes drawing and painting. Ask children to rewrite the sentence replacing the word 'likes' with a suitable synonym from the thesaurus. Discuss the nuances of meaning in the synonyms children have selected.

- Give out copies of the printable page 'Vocabulary upgrade' and give children time to complete it individually or in pairs.

Differentiation

Support: Help children to select an appropriate synonym by sitting them with an adult who can talk with them about the nuances of meaning in the words in the thesaurus.
Extension: Ask children to choose a short extract from *Goodnight Mister Tom* consisting of two or three sentences. Challenge them to rewrite the extract, replacing as many words as possible with synonyms.

Likely language

- When we want to talk or write about how likely something is, we use modal verbs and adverbials. For example:

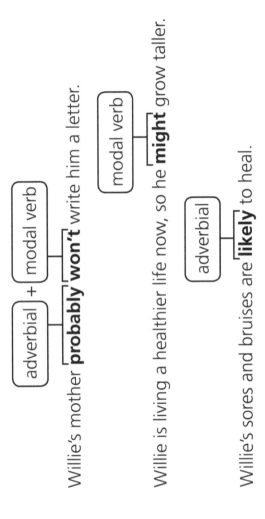

Willie's mother **probably won't** write him a letter.

Willie is living a healthier life now, so he **might** grow taller.

Willie's sores and bruises are **likely** to heal.

- The table below highlights language you can use to show the probability of something happening in the future. Modal verbs are written in italics and adverbials are written in normal text.

Degree of probability	IMPOSSIBLE	UNLIKELY	POSSIBLE	PROBABLE	CERTAIN
Language used (*Modal verbs* and adverbials)	*won't* *couldn't* definitely *won't* *couldn't* possibly	probably *won't* unlikely to not likely to	perhaps will maybe will possibly will *might* *could* *may*	probably will likely to	definitely will *will*

Sensible suffixes

'able' and 'ably':
- used if there is a related word ending in 'ation'.
- usually used if a complete root word can be heard before them.
- if added to a word ending in 'ce' or 'ge', the 'e' is kept.

'ible' and 'ibly':
- usually used when a complete root word can't be heard before them. However, there are a few exceptions (most notably 'sensible').

- Use the spelling rules above to circle the correct spelling from the two words in bold in each of the sentences below.

1. They built the shelter a **reasonible / reasonable** distance from the toilet.

2. It was so peaceful in Little Weirwold it didn't seem **possable / possible** there was a war on.

3. Tom asked Miss Thorne to suggest a **suitable / suitible** book for Willie.

4. Willie felt **miserable / miserible** because Sammy won the race.

5. Tom made Willie **comfortible / comfortable** in the armchair.

6. Sometimes, Willie wished he were **invisable / invisible**.

7. Willie's mother told him dogs were **horrible / horrable**.

8. Willie had a **terrable / terrible** pain in his stomach.

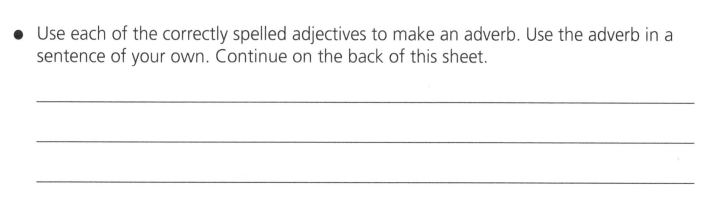

- Use each of the correctly spelled adjectives to make an adverb. Use the adverb in a sentence of your own. Continue on the back of this sheet.

_____

_____

_____

_____

Classy clauses

- Cut out the independent clauses below.
- Match each independent clause A with the correct independent clause B.
- Write each pair of matched clauses as a single sentence, punctuating the sentence correctly.

✂

A: everyone knew Tom was a widower

A: it was obvious Willie came from a deprived background

A: the doctor said Willie was malnourished

A: Willie was overcome by drowsiness

A: Willie couldn't believe his luck

A: Willie wouldn't take his jumper off

B: he fell asleep in the back of the cart

B: his wife had died forty years ago

B: he was too ashamed of his bruises

B: he was given a sweet and a comic

B: he had never slept in a bed before

B: he recommended easily digestible food, rest and exercise

1. Friday

Objective

To understand what they read.

What you need

Copies of *Goodnight Mister Tom*, photocopiable page 29 'Friday', interactive activity 'Friday Q & A', computers.

What to do

- Tell the children they are going to answer some questions about one particular chapter of the book: Chapter 11 'Friday'. (Wait until the whole class has read this chapter before doing this activity.)

- Give out copies of *Goodnight Mister Tom* and photocopiable page 29 'Friday'. Advise the children to read all the questions first, and then read the chapter with the questions in mind.

- Ask the children to tackle the questions one at a time, skimming the text for clues about where to find the answer, giving an appropriate amount of detail in their written response. If they get stuck on a question, they should move onto the next one and come back to it at the end.

- Give children a set time in which to answer as many questions as they can. When the time limit is up, discuss the questions and answers together.

- Complete the interactive activity 'Friday Q & A' as a whole class, in pairs or individually.

Differentiation

Support: Give children the task of answering selected questions only. Read through these questions with them, ensuring they understand them fully.

Extension: Encourage children to give more developed answers; for example, by including multiple direct references to the text and/or explaining their reasoning fully.

2. To cut a long story short

Objective

To précis longer passages.

What you need

Copies of *Goodnight Mister Tom*, photocopiable page 30 'To cut a long story short', computers (optional).

What to do

- Give out copies of *Goodnight Mister Tom* and photocopiable page 30 'To cut a long story short', which summarises one of the chapters in the novel. Ask children which chapter it is (Chapter 14, 'New Beginnings').

- Get children, working in pairs, to compare the précis with the original chapter (it is much shorter, written in present tense, no dialogue).

- Work with the class to choose a chapter (or part of a chapter) you have already read and write a précis of it within a set word limit (for example, 100 words). Discuss each stage of the process: skimming the text with the purpose of identifying and noting main events; expanding notes into full sentences; linking sentences; checking for sense; counting the number of words; redrafting; proofreading for spelling and punctuation errors; producing a final draft. Create a numbered list of these eight steps on the board.

- Challenge children to use the techniques they have been practising to write a précis of another chapter (or part of a chapter) of their own choice. A word processing program may help for this activity, as it will speed up the redrafting process.

Differentiation

Support: Group the children who may need support together and work with them to identify and note the main events in their chosen chapter (or part chapter) before they write their précis.

Extension: Challenge children to write a précis of the entire novel within a given word limit, for example, 250 words.

3. Open-ended

Objective

To assess the effectiveness of their own and others' writing.

What you need

Copies of *Goodnight Mister Tom*.

What to do

- Read the last few paragraphs of Chapter 22, from 'As Will lay back in his bed that night…'. Ask: *Could this have been the end of the story?*

- Ask: *Why do you think the final chapter is titled 'Postscript'?* (because the story was effectively wrapped up in the previous chapter)

- Read the final pages of Chapter 23 together (from '"Do you think," said Will…'). Ask: *Do you think this makes a better ending than the previous chapter would have done? Why?* or *Why not?*

- Ask: *Could you come up with a more effective ending?* Organise the class into pairs and ask children to discuss other possible endings with their partner.

- Get children to rewrite the ending of *Goodnight Mister Tom* using one of the ideas they discussed with their partner, or another idea.

- When they have finished writing their endings, invite children to swap work with a different partner, assess the effectiveness of each other's writing and give one another verbal feedback. Encourage children to revise and refine their endings in the light of the feedback they receive.

- If you have time, invite selected children to share their endings with the rest of the class.

Differentiation

Support: Ask children to plan out their ending by writing brief notes, and then use the notes to tell the story verbally to a classmate.
Extension: Encourage children to study the opening pages of the novel and write an alternative first scene.

4. People and places

Objective

To draw inferences.

What you need

Copies of *Goodnight Mister Tom*.

What to do

- Revise the term 'setting' (where the action in a narrative takes place). Ask pairs or small groups to make a list of the settings in *Goodnight Mister Tom*.

- Discuss how setting affects the emotions of the characters (for example, Willie feels safe in Little Weirwold; the children feel frightened when they approach Spooky Cott; Tom feels ill at ease in London).

- Establish that some settings can tell you something about a character, such as Tom's bedroom (Chapter 1), Zach's bedroom (Chapter 10), Willie's bedroom (Chapter 11), Mrs Beech's front room (Chapter 15) or Geoffrey's hideout (Chapter 20).

- Choose one of these settings and read the passage describing it. Ask: *What can you tell about this person's character from their room?*

- Get pairs to discuss what a different character's room might be like (for example, George's or Carrie's), drawing inferences from what they know about the person's character.

- Challenge children to write a description of George's or Carrie's room or another setting associated with one of the other characters.

- Ask children to share their written descriptions. They should be prepared to justify what they have written using inference from what they know about the related character.

Differentiation

Support: Provide children with a word bank containing vocabulary that could be used to describe George's or Carrie's room.
Extension: Ask children to think of examples from other books they have read in which settings reveal something about character.

5. What's it all about?

Objective

To identify and discuss themes.

What you need

Copies of *Goodnight Mister Tom*, photocopiable page 31 'What's it all about?', interactive activity 'Identifying themes' (Extension activity).

Cross-curricular link

PSHE

What to do

- Ask: *What is* Goodnight Mister Tom *about?* Get children to discuss this question with a partner and write an answer in no more than 20 words (for example, an abused boy who is sent to live with an elderly widower and is healed by his love and care). Ask the children to repeat the exercise using no more than 10 words (for example, a boy who is healed) and finally just one word (for example, healing).

- Explain that these one-word answers reflect what the story is about at the deepest level – its themes. Themes can often be expressed using a single word – usually an abstract noun, such as healing.

- Using the theme of healing as an example, ask: *What messages does the author communicate through this theme?* (For example, that healing is possible or that love promotes healing.)

- Organise the class into groups, giving each group a copy of photocopiable page 31 'What's it all about?'. Ask groups to discuss the questions fully before writing their answers.

- Share ideas as a whole class.

Differentiation

Support: Before working on the task from the photocopiable sheet, get children to consider familiar stories, such as fairy tales, and identify their themes. Refer to the list of common themes on the photocopiable sheet to help.

Extension: Challenge children to complete the interactive activity 'Identifying themes'.

6. Language effects

Objective

To evaluate how authors use language, considering the impact on the reader.

What you need

Copies of *Goodnight Mister Tom*, printable page 'Language features'.

What to do

- Ask: *What makes* Goodnight Mister Tom *enjoyable?* Identify various aspects that contribute to children's enjoyment of the story, including characters, events and language.

- Tell children that in this lesson they will be examining how the language the author uses helps to make the book enjoyable.

- Display the printable page 'Language features'. Discuss the language features listed in the table, ensuring children understand what each one means.

- Give out copies of *Goodnight Mister Tom*. Choose one of the language features on the printable page and ask children to find an example of it in the text. Discuss what effect the use of this language feature has and how it adds to the reader's enjoyment of the story.

- Organise children into pairs, giving each pair a copy of the printable page 'Language features' to complete.

- Discuss the following question with the whole class: *Which language features contribute most to your enjoyment of the story? Why?*

Differentiation

Support: In the paired activity, ask children to look through a specific chapter (or part of a chapter) for any of the listed language features, rather than the whole text.

Extension: Ask children to discuss the following question in pairs or small groups: *Which do you think plays the biggest role in making* Goodnight Mister Tom *enjoyable: the characters, the events or the language? Explain your answer.*

7. A question of time

Objective

To make comparisons within and across books.

What you need

Copies of *Goodnight Mister Tom*, copies of other familiar fiction books.

What to do

- Tell the children that in this lesson they will be considering the novel's setting, not in terms of place, but in terms of time. Ask: *When is* Goodnight Mister Tom *set?* (World War II; specifically the first year of the war, from 1939 to 1940)

- Get children, working in small groups, to identify and discuss aspects of the novel in which the historical period the novel is set in makes a difference to the story.

- Invite groups to report back on their discussions. Make a list on the board of the aspects of the story they have identified. Ask: *Why do you think the author chose to set the story at the beginning of World War II?*

- Ask children to suggest how these aspects of the story may have been different if the novel had been set during a different period in history, for example, in the present day. Ask: *Would the story have worked as well?*

- Ask children to choose other fiction books they have read and discuss in their group how the time in which they are set (time of year, time of day or historical period) contributes to the story.

Differentiation

Support: During group work, group less confident learners together, sit with them and help to steer their discussion.

Extension: Ask children to write a report with one of the following titles: 'Why *Goodnight Mister Tom* is set in 1939 to 1940' or 'How *Goodnight Mister Tom* would be different if it were set in the present day'.

8. Plotting the plot

Objective

To discuss and identify plot conventions.

What you need

Interactive activity 'Order, order!', copies of *Goodnight Mister Tom*, printable page 'Plotting the plot'.

What to do

- Display the interactive activity 'Order, order!', asking children to move the various events from *Goodnight Mister Tom* into the correct order.

- Ask: *What is the term used to describe the sequence of events in a story?* (the plot)

- Remind children that the standard plot structure consists of four phases. Challenge them, working in pairs, to write these four phases. Depending on the children's prior knowledge, you may want to give them an out-of-sequence list of plot phases to order (for example, climax, conflict, exposition, resolution).

- Establish the correct order of the plot phases (1. exposition 2. conflict 3. climax 4. resolution) and ask children to explain each phase. (The exposition phase introduces the characters and the setting; the conflict phase introduces one or more problems; the climax phase is the turning point in the story (the point at which things change); and the resolution is the ending.)

- Ask: *Does* Goodnight Mister Tom *fit standard plot structure?* Ask the children to use printable page 'Plotting the plot' to summarise the main events in the story and to fit different chapters to the different phases.

- Discuss how closely the plot of *Goodnight Mister Tom* fits standard plot structure.

Differentiation

Support: Group the children who may need support together and work with them to help them complete the printable sheet.

Extension: Ask children to compare and contrast the plot structure of *Goodnight Mister Tom* with another story they have read.

Friday

- Answer these questions about Chapter 11, 'Friday'.

1. Explain one way in which Tom has changed since Willie's arrival.

_____

2. Does George like school? How do you know?

_____

_____

3. State two things Carrie is angry about.

_____

_____

4. What prompts Carrie to say to Zach, *'Now you know how I feel...'*?

_____

_____

_____

5. What clues are we given near the end of the chapter that Willie's recovery is almost complete?

_____

_____

_____

6. How does the author create humour in this chapter?

_____

_____

_____

_____

To cut a long story short

- The text below summarises one of the chapters of *Goodnight Mister Tom*. Read the text and identify the chapter it summarises.

In January Willie leaves Mrs Black's class and starts in Mrs Hartridge's class. Carrie asks Mrs Hartridge if she can take the exam for high school and Mrs Hartridge tells her she'll think about it.

By March Willie is happily settled into his new class and Carrie is making progress towards taking the high school exam. Willie, Zach, George and the twins meet in Zach's room and discuss their plans for an expedition to Spooky Cott.

Tom receives a letter from Willie's mother: she's ill and wants Willie to go back home.

- With a partner compare the text above with the chapter it summarises. Discuss the differences. Use the space below to make notes.

What's it all about?

- Which of the themes in the list below are important in *Goodnight Mister Tom*. Discuss this question in your group and circle the themes you identify.

beauty	fate	loneliness
betrayal	forgiveness	loss
bravery	friendship	love
change	healing	prejudice
death	honesty	religion
dreams	identity	revenge
family	justice	strength

- Are there any other themes you think are important in *Goodnight Mister Tom*? Discuss this question in your group and note your ideas below.

▼ TALK ABOUT IT

1. Serious stuff

Objective

To give well-structured descriptions and explanations for different purposes, including for expressing feelings.

What you need

Copies of *Goodnight Mister Tom*.

Cross-curricular link

PSHE

What to do

- Establish that problems are an important element in the plot of any story. Ask: *What problems do the characters in* Goodnight Mister Tom *face?*

- Children may identify a range of problems such as neglect, abuse, poor physical health, injury, poor mental health, illiteracy, bereavement, displacement, loneliness and prejudice.

- Choose one issue to discuss in more depth (for example, prejudice). Ask children to identify specific examples of that issue in *Goodnight Mister Tom* (for example, Carrie getting picked on at High School because of her accent, Mrs Beech getting angry at Willie for being friends with a Jewish boy). Ask: *How might these examples make the character feel?*

- Ask groups to discuss the following questions: *Why do you think the author included this issue in the novel? What was she trying to say about it?*

- Come back together as a class for children to share the ideas they've been discussing.

- Make yourself available immediately after the lesson for any children who want to talk to you privately about any of the issues you have been discussing.

Differentiation

Support: Sit with the group that needs the most support with the discussion activity and help to steer their discussion.
Extension: Ask groups to discuss the advice they would give to a character in the story about one of the problems they are facing.

2. Missing pages

Objective

To use spoken language to develop understanding through hypothesising, imagining and exploring ideas.

What you need

Copies of *Goodnight Mister Tom*.

What to do

- Ideally, wait until children have read the whole book before you do this activity.

- Explain that in a novel an author cannot possibly tell every part of the story in detail; that some parts of the story take place 'off the page' in 'missing pages'.

- Through paired discussion, ask children to identify places in the book where there might be 'missing pages', and, in general terms, what these missing pages might be about (for example, there might be missing pages in Chapter 21 about Zach's trip to London).

- Invite children to share the results of the paired discussion with the whole class, encouraging as many children as possible to contribute. Note some or all of the missing pages suggestions on the board.

- Changing discussion partners, ask children to choose one of the missing pages ideas and work out with their partner the details of what happens in these missing pages.

- Come back together as a class to share and discuss ideas.

- You could use this activity as a springboard for a writing activity in which children write the missing pages.

Differentiation

Support: Pair less confident learners with a more confident partner.
Extension: Challenge pairs to form their ideas into a cohesive narrative and then tell it aloud to the class.

3. Improvise it!

Objective

To participate in role play and improvisation.

What you need

Copies of *Goodnight Mister Tom*.

What to do

- Ask children to discuss their favourite scenes from *Goodnight Mister Tom*. Ask: *Which scenes do you think would be the most interesting to act out? Why?*

- Organise the children into groups. Ask each group to choose a scene from *Goodnight Mister Tom* and create a 'freeze frame' (like a photograph), communicating what's happening through facial expression and body language. Challenge the rest of the class to identify which scene each group has chosen.

- Invite groups to choose a different scene from the book and mime it (using movement but no sound, like a silent film). Challenge the rest of the class to identify each scene.

- Ask groups to improvise a scene that doesn't appear in the book (for example, Willie leaving home when he was evacuated, the death of Tom's wife Rachel or Carrie's first day at High School). Tell children that this time they can use both sound and movement.

- If you have the time, let groups perform their improvised scenes for the class, using simple costumes or props if appropriate.

Differentiation

Support: Help children draw out ideas for what might happen in their improvised scene through asking questions and encouraging discussion.
Extension: Invite children to perform an improvised monologue, role playing one of the characters and saying what they really think and feel about a particular event in the story.

4. Perfect presentations

Objective

To participate in presentations.

What you need

Photocopiable page 35 'Preparing an effective presentation', internet access, books about World War II (optional), video recording equipment (optional).

What to do

- Tell the children they will be preparing and giving a presentation about a topic related to World War II – the period during which *Goodnight Mister Tom* is set.

- Either give children the following list of topics to choose from, or ask them to come up with their own list of topics through class discussion. (Possible topics: the causes of the war, evacuation, the Blitz, air-raid shelters, schools, daily life, rationing, conscription.)

- Establish that an effective presentation has a set structure. Give out photocopiable page 35 'Preparing an effective presentation' and discuss the criteria it outlines.

- To collect information for their presentation, children will need to conduct research on the internet and/or in books. Discuss research techniques and also revise the school guidelines for staying safe online.

- Once children have prepared their presentations, discuss performance criteria for an effective presentation, such as ensuring appropriate volume, clarity, pace, intonation and eye contact.

- Invite children to give their presentations. Ask the class to assess each presentation in terms of the criteria they have been considering.

Differentiation

Support: Help children to prepare prompt cards to use during their presentation.
Extension: Challenge children to make video recordings of each other's presentations and share them with a wider audience.

5. In the hot seat

Objective

To ask relevant questions to extend their understanding and knowledge.

What you need

Photocopiable page 36 'Hot-seat questions', simple costumes or props to denote the main characters in *Goodnight Mister Tom* (optional).

What to do

- Ask: *Which of the characters from* Goodnight Mister Tom *would you most like to meet? Why?* Give children time to discuss these questions in pairs or small groups.

- Come back together as a class and share ideas. Establish the two characters children would most like to meet. Tell children they will have an opportunity to 'meet' these characters and ask them questions.

- Ask for volunteers to take the parts of each of the two characters in a hot-seating question and answer session. Choose children you are confident will cope well with the demands of the activity.

- Give out copies of photocopiable page 36 'Hot-seat questions'. Give children time to make notes on the photocopiable sheet of questions they would like to ask the two characters.

- Help the children who will be sitting in the hot seat to think about the sorts of questions they might be asked and how they will respond. Perhaps give them simple costumes or props for the characters they will be playing.

- Lead the hot-seating question and answer session or ask a volunteer to lead it.

Differentiation

Support: Pair less confident learners with a more confident partner.
Extension: Ask the children who played the hot-seat characters to come out of character and share their experience of doing the activity with the rest of the class.

6. What's next?

Objective

To give well-structured narratives.

What you need

Photocopiable page 37 'Planning a sequel to *Goodnight Mister Tom*'.

What to do

- Revise the term 'sequel': a narrative (for example, book or film) that continues the story started in an existing narrative.

- Invite children to imagine that there is a sequel to *Goodnight Mister Tom*. Ask: *What do you think happens in the sequel?* Get children to discuss initial ideas with a partner.

- Tell children they will be working individually to plan their own sequel and then telling the story of the sequel to a group. Ask children to complete photocopiable page 37 'Planning a sequel to *Goodnight Mister Tom*', which guides them in outlining the sequel's plot.

- Discuss rules and tips for speaking and listening in a group (for example, only one person speaks at a time, keep listeners engaged by using expression, and so on).

- Organise the class into groups of three or four. Ask children to use their notes from the photocopiable sheet to help them tell their story to their group.

- Choose selected children to tell their stories to the class.

Differentiation

Support: Children could complete the photocopiable sheet with a partner and share the storytelling with them.
Extension: Ask children to give an oral retelling of the story of *Goodnight Mister Tom* to another class.

Preparing an effective presentation

● Use these tips to help you prepare an effective presentation.

Structure
An effective presentation has a three-part structure: an introduction, a main body and a conclusion.

Introduction
● Start with something to grab listeners' interest – such as a question or a quotation.
● Expand on the title – explains what the presentation will be about in more detail.

Main body
● Make a series of points.
● The points should be organised so that they are in a logical order. This is especially important if the presentation contains instructions.

Conclusion
● Sum up the presentation.
● If the presentation started with a question, finish the presentation by asking it again and then giving the answer.

Notes
The purpose of giving the presentation is to practise your speaking skills, not your reading skills.

For this reason you will not be writing your presentation down. However, you may want to make notes to help you remember what you want to talk about.

Tips for making notes:
● Make brief notes only – just key words and phrases.
● Use a separate piece of paper or card for each point you want to make.
● Number your pieces of paper or card to show their order.

Hot-seat questions

● Write some questions you would like to ask each hot-seat character. Use the question starters below to give you ideas.

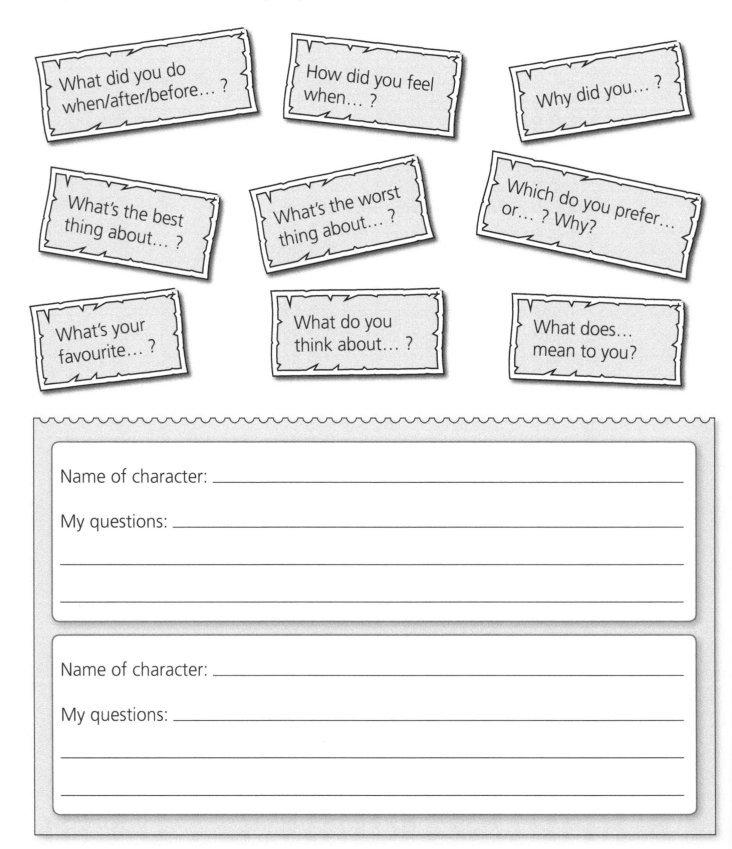

What did you do when/after/before… ?

How did you feel when… ?

Why did you… ?

What's the best thing about… ?

What's the worst thing about… ?

Which do you prefer… or… ? Why?

What's your favourite… ?

What do you think about… ?

What does… mean to you?

Name of character: _____

My questions: _____

_____

_____

Name of character: _____

My questions: _____

_____

_____

Planning a sequel to *Goodnight Mister Tom*

- Imagine that there is a sequel to *Goodnight Mister Tom*. You are going to tell the story of the sequel to a group.
- Use this page to plan the story. You will be able to refer to it when you are telling the story.

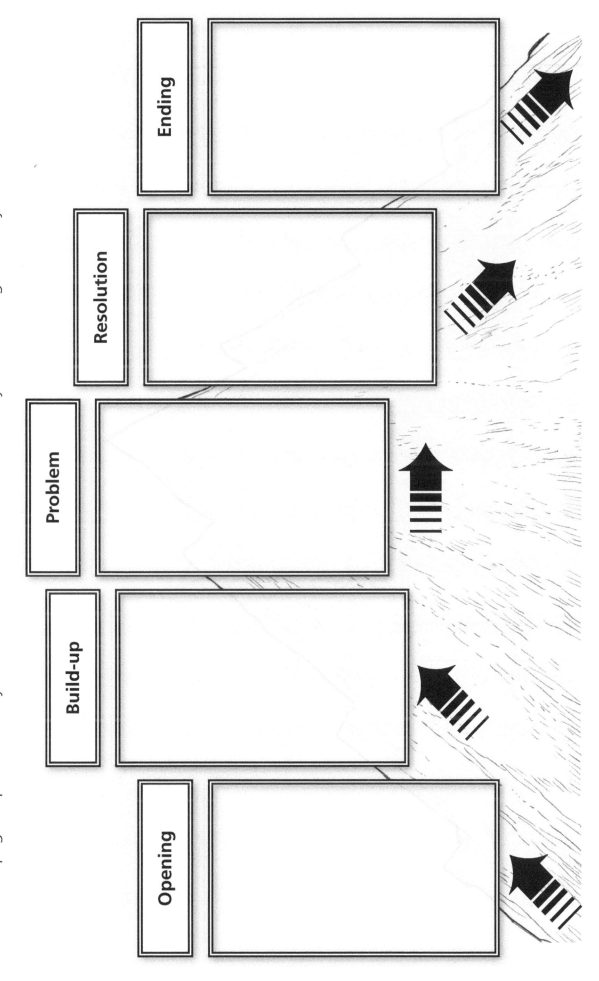

Opening

Build-up

Problem

Resolution

Ending

GET WRITING

1. Letters home

Objective

To plan writing by identifying the audience and purpose.

What you need

Copies of *Goodnight Mister Tom*, printable page 'Letter template' (Support only).

What to do

- Together read the following passages from *Goodnight Mister Tom* about the King children:
  - towards the end of Chapter 11: from 'I don't think Christine and Robert King are very happy…' to '…if they didn't work hard enuff.'
  - around the middle of Chapter 12: the whole of the paragraph beginning 'I'm afraid I've just had some rather bad news.'

- Ask: *How might Christine and Robert's mother have found out they were unhappy at Hillbrook Farm?* (Robert and Christine probably wrote to tell her.)

- Ask children to imagine they are Christine or Robert and they want to write a letter to persuade their mother to take them back home.

- Recap the features of a letter. Ask: *What purpose will this letter have?* (to persuade) Ask children to describe features commonly used in persuasive texts, such as only telling one side of the story and using emotive language for emphasis.

- Ask: *How will the audience for this letter affect the way it is written?* (The audience is the children's mother so it will use informal layout and language.)

- Ask children to write the letter including all the information from the extracts you have read and using their imaginations to provide additional details.

Differentiation

Support: Provide children with printable page 'Letter template'.
Extension: Challenge children to write a short play depicting what happens when Christine and Robert's mother arrives to take them home.

2. It was a rainy night…

Objective

To use tenses consistently and correctly throughout a piece of writing.

What you need

Interactive activity 'Don't get tense over tenses', copies of *Goodnight Mister Tom*.

What to do

- Discuss why it is important to use the correct tenses when writing. Play the interactive activity 'Don't get tense over tenses'.

- Give out copies of *Goodnight Mister Tom*. Read the description of Will's painting 'A Rainy Night' in Chapter 14, from 'The painting was set at night…' to 'They were eyeing the money in the cap.'

- Ask children to plan the plot of a story that starts 'It was a rainy night…'. Their story could be based on Will's painting, or it could be based on an idea of their own. Tell them to use whichever planning format they prefer (for example, story mountain, spider diagram or timeline). As well as the story structure, also ask them to consider the style, setting and characters.

- Ask children to write the opening paragraph of their story. Emphasise that they want readers to carry on reading, so they should make the opening paragraph exciting and make it easy to read and understand (for example, by ensuring their verb tenses are consistent and correct).

- Ask children to swap opening paragraphs with a friend and revise their writing in response to feedback.

Differentiation

Support: You could provide children with a template on which to plan their story and/or a rainy night-related word bank.
Extension: Ask children to write the closing paragraph of the story, again ensuring correct use of tenses. Challenge them to link the final paragraph to the opening paragraph in some way.

3. Rescue!

Objective

To use a wide range of devices to build cohesion within and across paragraphs.

What you need

Photocopiable page 43 'Rescue!', copies of *Goodnight Mister Tom*, interactive activities 'Connective crunch' and 'Cohesive conundrum'.

What to do

- Ask: *What does it mean if we say a text is cohesive? Why is it important for a text to be cohesive? Can you name any cohesive devices?* Make a list of categories of cohesive device on the board:
  - pronouns, the definite article (both of these referring back to nouns that have already been mentioned)
  - repetition (for effect)
  - ellipsis (missed out words that are understood from previous content)
  - synonyms (to avoid repetition)
  - connectives.

- Give out copies of *Goodnight Mister Tom* and together read a short passage from Chapter 17, 'Rescue'. Choose a passage that is mainly narration rather than dialogue. Ask children to identify the cohesive devices in the passage you have read. Discuss ideas.

- Give out photocopiable page 43 'Rescue!', which lists the main events of Chapter 17.

- Ask children to use the information on the photocopiable sheet to write a summary of Chapter 17, incorporating a range of cohesive devices in their writing. You might want to give children an approximate word count to aim for.

Differentiation

Support: Introduce the interactive activity 'Connective crunch', and challenge children to complete it either individually or in pairs.
Extension: Challenge individuals working independently to complete the interactive activity 'Cohesive conundrum'.

4. Put it right

Objective

To proofread for spelling and punctuation errors.

What you need

Photocopiable page 41 'Put it right', photocopiable page 42 'All right now', copies of *Goodnight Mister Tom*, interactive activity 'Put it right' (Support only).

What to do

- Discuss why it is important to proofread your writing for spelling and punctuation errors. Give out photocopiable page 41 'Put it right', which asks children to correct errors of spelling and punctuation in a short passage. Ask children to complete the photocopiable sheet individually.

- Give out copies of photocopiable page 42 'All right now' which gives the correct version of the text from page 41.

- Ask children to swap copies of photocopiable page 41 with a partner and use photocopiable page 42 to check each other's work.

- Working in pairs, ask one child to dictate a short passage from *Goodnight Mister Tom* for their partner to write down and then proofread. Partners should then swap roles and finally check each other's work. You might want to specify a maximum length for the passages children choose, for example, thirty words or two sentences. You might also want to ask children to avoid dialogue involving non-standard English, as this will be difficult for their partner to spell correctly.

Differentiation

Support: Instead of giving children the photocopiable sheet, provide them with simpler errors to correct by getting them to complete the interactive activity 'Put it right'.
Extension: Ask children to write additional questions in the style of those on the photocopiable sheet and give them to a partner to complete.

5. Creating atmosphere

Objective

To select grammar and vocabulary to enhance meaning.

What you need

Copies of *Goodnight Mister Tom*.

What to do

- Together read one or more descriptions of places from *Goodnight Mister Tom*, such as the description of Salmouth from Chapter 19, or the description of Spooky Cott from Chapter 20.

- After reading each description, ask: *What sort of atmosphere does the author create? How does she create it?* Identify and discuss the grammar and vocabulary choices that help the author to create the desired atmosphere.

- Ask children to think about a particular place that has a distinct atmosphere. This might be a place in *Goodnight Mister Tom*, a real place they know well or a place that exists only in their imagination.

- Encourage children to describe the place they want to write about to a partner.

- Challenge children to write a description of their chosen place, selecting grammar and vocabulary to enhance meaning and contribute to atmosphere.

- Ask children to pair up with a different partner and read each other their descriptions. Can they guess what sort of atmosphere their partner is trying to create? How successful were they?

Differentiation

Support: Ask children to make their written descriptions very short (two or three sentences) and focus the challenge on the quality of their writing, not the quantity.

Extension: Ask children to find and discuss effective descriptions of places from other books they have read.

6. The play's the thing

Objective

To perform their own compositions with appropriate intonation, volume and movement.

What you need

Copies of *Goodnight Mister Tom*, printable pages 'The beginning'.

What to do

- Ask children to think about the settings in the story – the places where the action takes place. Working in pairs or small groups, ask them to list as many settings as they can within a given time limit (for example, three minutes).

- Ask children to imagine they are writing a stage play of the story and only a limited number of sets can be built (for example, four). Ask: *Which four settings would you choose for your sets?* Get children to discuss this question in pairs or small groups and then justify their reasoning to the class.

- Together, read the play script from printable page 'The beginning'. Compare the play script to the equivalent passage in the novel (Chapter 1). Ask: *In what ways has the novel been changed to create the play script?*

- Divide the class into groups, giving each group a different scene from the book to rewrite as a play script (ensuring they follow the conventions of a written script).

- Get groups to perform their play scripts in front of the class using appropriate intonation, volume and movement.

Differentiation

Support: Encourage children to refer closely to the novel while writing their play script, selecting existing sentences and linking them with their own words.

Extension: Ask children not to refer to the novel too much while writing their play script. Instead, encourage them to write in the style of the novel using their own words.

Put it right

- The passage below contains some errors in spelling and some of the capital letters and punctuation marks are missing.
- Draw a line like this —— through any misspelled words. Write the correct spelling above.
- Circle where a capital letter or punctuation mark is missing. Write the correct capital letter or punctuation mark above.

Ever since it was frist published in 1981, *Goodnite*

Mister Tom has been hailed as a modun classic.

Set agenst the backdrop of the early days of

World War II, its a powerfull and tuching story

about human relasionships and the heeling power

of love

The story has bin adapted multiple times for

the radio the theatre as both a play and a musical)

and, in 1998, as a TV film staring the late

John thaw the film adaptation one seven televison

awards, including a BAFTA.

All right now

- Below is the corrected version of the passage from 'Put it right'. You are going to use it to check your partner's work.
- Tick each error your partner corrected.
- Count up the ticks to give your partner a mark out of 20.

Ever since it was <u>first</u> published in 1981, *Goodnight Mister Tom* has been hailed as a <u>modern</u> classic. Set <u>against</u> the backdrop of the early days of World War II, <u>it's</u> a <u>powerful</u> and <u>touching</u> story about human <u>relationships</u> and the <u>healing</u> power of love<u>.</u>

The story has <u>been</u> adapted multiple times<u>:</u> for the radio<u>,</u> the theatre (as both a play and a musical) and, in 1998, as a TV film <u>starring</u> the late John <u>Thaw. T</u>he film adaptation <u>won</u> seven <u>television</u> awards, including a BAFTA.

Rescue!

- Below is a list of the main events in Chapter 17, 'Rescue'.
- Use the list to help you write a summary of Chapter 17. Use a range of cohesive devices in your writing.

The main events in Chapter 17

- Tom finds Will tied up under the stairs clutching a bundle.

- An ambulance collects them.

- Tom takes the bundle from Will and sees the baby is dead.

- Will is taken to the children's ward.

- Will is having nightmares and being sedated. He asks to go back with Tom.

- Tom finds out Will is going to be sent to a children's home.

- Tom decides to kidnap Will.

- Tom bundles Will into a blanket and carries him out.

- The warden spots Tom carrying Will out of the hospital. He wishes him luck.

- Tom, Will and Sammy spend the night at the train station.

- They get a train to Skyron.

- From Skyron they get three lifts.

- Tom walks the next five miles to the blacksmith's.

- Tom drives the cart to Little Weirwold.

- Will wakes up on the cart then goes back to sleep.

- Tom takes Will to Doctor Little.

- Zach comes down and sees Will.

- Tom falls asleep.

ASSESSMENT

1. Have your say

To participate in a discussion about books they have read.

What you need

Copies of *Goodnight Mister Tom*.

What to do

- Tell children that in this lesson they will have the opportunity to discuss some of their opinions on *Goodnight Mister Tom* within a group.

- Remind children about your expectations of their behaviour when speaking and listening in a group (for example, only one person to speak at a time, listen respectfully and express opinions politely). Remind children that it's perfectly okay for there to be differences of opinion within a group, but that it's not okay for them to argue over these differences.

- On the board write some topics for discussion based on personal opinion about the whole book, for example, favourite character; least favourite character; funniest moment; saddest moment; biggest surprise; or best chapter. Give groups plenty of time for discussion, so that they can explore several of these topics. Assess individual children's attainment from their contribution to the discussion, drawing out more reticent speakers through questioning where needed.

- Bring the class back together, asking groups to share the most interesting points that came up in their discussion. Encourage children to explain and justify their opinions.

Differentiation

Extension: Ask children to devise and discuss additional opinion-related questions about *Goodnight Mister Tom*.

2. Dear Ms Magorian...

Objective

To propose changes to vocabulary, grammar and punctuation to enhance effects and clarify meaning.

What you need

Computers (optional).

What to do

- Ask children to imagine they could talk to Michelle Magorian, the author of *Goodnight Mister Tom*. Ask: *What would you want to tell her? What would you want to ask her?*

- Get children to discuss their questions in pairs or small groups and then report back to the class. Tell children they will be writing a letter to Michelle Magorian.

- Revise the features of formal letters, including address and date placement, and options for starting and ending the letter.

- Ask children to write the first draft of their letter independently. This stage offers an opportunity for assessing each child's understanding of the novel.

- Assign each child a writing partner. Encourage partners to help each other improve their drafts by editing vocabulary, grammar and punctuation. This stage offers an opportunity to assess individuals against the lesson objective.

- Ask children to create a final draft of their letter.

Differentiation

Support: Provide children with a word bank of suitable phrases to include in their letter.

3. Writing reviews

Objective

To recommend books they have read.

What you need

Media resource 'Book review'.

What to do

- Tell the children they will be writing a review of *Goodnight Mister Tom* which they will then share with others (for example, via the school learning platform, the public library, or email correspondence).

- Display and discuss the media resource 'Book review'. Ask: *How do these reviews differ from one another? What do they have in common? Who is the intended audience? How do you know? Which review would you find most useful? Why?*

- Ask: *What will you include in your book review of* Goodnight Mister Tom? Get children discussing this question in groups. Ask groups further questions to help them clarify what they will write; for example, *How much of the plot will you give away? Will you use a scoring system? If so, which type? Who will you share your book review with and how will you share it? How will this influence what you write and how you present it?*

- Get children to plan, write and revise their book reviews independently. You can then assess each completed book review against the lesson objective. Involve children in the process of distributing their book reviews to the intended audience.

Differentiation

Support: Ask children to base the format of their review on one of the sample reviews from the media resource.
Extension: Challenge children to read one of Michelle Magorian's other novels and present an oral review to the rest of the class.

4. What do you think?

Objective

To draw inferences.

What you need

Photocopiable page 47 'What do you think?'.

What to do

- Tell the children they are going to answer some questions that will require them to think about the novel *Goodnight Mister Tom* as a whole.

- Give out copies of photocopiable page 47 'What do you think?'. Tell children that as this is an assessment, it is an opportunity to show you what they have understood, so they need to work independently.

- Advise the children to:
  - Read all the questions before they attempt to answer any of them.
  - Start with whichever question they think they will find the easiest to answer; there is no need to attempt the questions in order.
  - Move onto another question if they get stuck and come back to the original question later if they have time.
  - Answer questions as fully as they can.

- Give children a set time in which to answer as many of the comprehension questions as they can. When the time is up, take in their work.

- Finally, display a copy of the photocopiable sheet and discuss the questions and answers together.

Differentiation

Support: Give children who may need support some extra help by reading through the questions with them, ensuring they understand them fully.
Extension: Ask children to devise their own question(s) about the book as a whole, similar to those on the photocopiable sheet, and discuss it/them with a friend.

5. Debate it!

Objective

To explain and discuss their understanding of what they have read through formal debate.

What you need

Writing materials.

What to do

- Provide a controversial motion for a class debate based on *Goodnight Mister Tom*, such as: It was wrong for Tom to kidnap Will.

- Divide the class into two equal teams: one to propose the motion and one to oppose it. It's advisable to allocate children to teams randomly.

- Divide each team into smaller groups in order to prepare their arguments. Encourage communication between groups on the same team to ensure arguments are not duplicated.

- Choose a moderator to lead the debate. You could do this yourself or select a child for the role. When all the arguments have been prepared, the moderator introduces the motion and invites representatives from each team to present their arguments, alternating between the two teams.

- After the prepared arguments have been presented, give teams the opportunity to prepare and present rebuttals in response to the opposing side's arguments.

- Complete the debate by asking children to vote for the point of view that was supported by the most compelling arguments. Assess individuals against how well they participated in the debate.

Differentiation

Extension: During the debate, ask one or two children to keep notes summarising the arguments on each side and ask them to provide a quick recap before the vote.

6. Questions, questions!

Objective

To ask relevant questions to improve their understanding.

What you need

Copies of *Goodnight Mister Tom* (optional).

What to do

- Ensure all children have finished reading the novel before you conduct this activity.

- Explain that it's not possible for an author to explain absolutely everything in a novel. Ask children to suggest why this is the case (for example, it would complicate the plot too much; it would make the novel too long; it would interrupt the flow; it would be boring).

- Tell children that during this activity they will be identifying some of the unanswered questions in the novel.

- Ask children to give you a list of question words. Write them on the board (Who, Where, When, Why, What, Which, How).

- Ask: *What unanswered questions do you have about* Goodnight Mister Tom? Get children to discuss this in pairs or small groups, and make a note of the questions they have.

- Bring the class back together, asking children to share their unanswered questions. Discuss what the answers might be and why.

- Use the questions asked as well as the answers given to assess individual children's understanding of the novel.

What do you think?

- Answer these questions as fully as you can.

1. Why do you think Will is so fascinated with Zach?

_____

_____

_____

_____

2. Will changes a lot. What do you think is the main reason for this change?

_____

_____

_____

_____

3. Why do you think the author 'killed off' Will's mother?

_____

_____

_____

_____

5. What do you think is the most important message in *Goodnight Mister Tom*?

_____

_____

_____

_____

Available in this series:

978-1407-16055-9

978-1407-16056-6

978-1407-16057-3

978-1407-16058-0

978-1407-16059-7

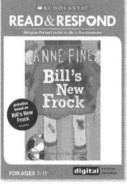

978-1407-16060-3

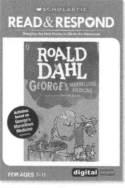

978-1407-16061-0

978-1407-16062-7

978-1407-16063-4

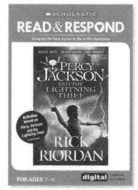

978-1407-16064-1

978-1407-16065-8

978-1407-16052-8

978-1407-16067-2

978-1407-16068-9

978-1407-16069-6

978-1407-16070-2

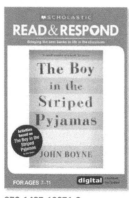

978-1407-16071-9

978-1407-17616-1

978-1407-17614-7

978-1407-17615-4

To find out more, call: 0845 6039091
or visit our website www.scholastic.co.uk/readandrespond